Vegetarian Christmas

THE 120 TASTIEST RECIPES
FOR THE
WINTER CHRISTMAS TIME!

Nadia Uzhakhova

All advice in this book has been carefully considered and checked by the author and the publisher. Nevertheless, no guarantee can be given. Any liability of the author or the publisher for any personal injury, property damage or financial loss is therefore excluded.

Vegetarian Christmas
Copyright © 2022 Nadia Uzhakhova

All rights reserved, in particular the right to reproduce and distribute the translation. No part of this work may be reproduced in any form (by photocopy, microfilm or any other process) or stored, processed, duplicated or distributed using electronic systems without the written permission of the publisher.

Edition 2022

Foreword

Welcome to this vegetarian cookbook. In this book, you will find a selection of the 120 best Christmas recipes.

Eating a vegetarian diet does not mean that you have to give up taste and variety. On the contrary! This form of nutrition offers countless opportunities to broaden one's horizons.

Here you get a great collection of different recipes for every part of the day and of course, you can also expand or modify them.

P. S: I have deliberately omitted pictures in order to keep the printing costs low and to be able to offer the book at a reasonable price.

I wish you good luck of course

Enjoy your meal!

Content

Vegetarian Christmas 1

Foreword 3

In advance - information about the recipes 9

Soups 10
   Red Lentil Coconut Soup 11
   Pumpkin soup 12
   Cheese soup 13
   Vegetable cream soup 14
   Tomatoes - Vegetables soup 15
   Broccoli cream soup 16
   Cauliflower soup 17
   Buckwheat - paprika soup 18
   Barley soup 19
   Chestnut cream soup 20
   Celery - Apple Soup 21
   Spicy orange lentil soup 22
   Sweet Potato Chickpea Soup 23
   Cream of mushroom soup 24
   Potato and leek soup 25

Main dishes 26
   Pancake 27
   South Tyrolean spinach dumplings 28
   Soy Schnitzel Viennese Style 30
   Veget. Minced meat stew 31
   Tomato-Lentil Stew 32
   Vegetable - coconut stew 34
   Pasta pan with mushrooms 35
   Smoked Tofu Casserole 36

- Oven vegetables...37
- Spinach - Risotto...38
- Pumpkin ragout..39
- Baked apple strudel with vanilla sauce..............................40
- Lentil-paranut roast..42
- Coconut spaghetti...44
- Baked Beans...45
- Potato gratin..46
- Pichelsteiner..47
- Grilled Corn on the cob..48
- Rice - meatballs..49
- Winter Ratatouille..50
- Chickpea curry...52
- Potato goulash...53
- Potato - Carrot Rösti..54
- Kohlrabi potato vegetables...55
- Grilled Pepper skewers..56
- Spaghetti with peanut sauce..57
- Grilled Mushroom skewers..58
- Paprika - Couscous..59
- Stuffed mushrooms..60
- Fried tofu...61

Sweets - Cookies 62

- Waffles...63
- Marzipan potatoes..64
- Mocha cookies..65
- Cinnamon stars..66
- Nut biscuits..68
- Marzipan nougat pralines..70
- Shortbread biscuits..71
- Coconut macaroons..72
- Chocolate pralines..73
- Speculoos...74

 Simple gingerbread..75
 Chocolate gingerbread...76
 Peppernuts..77
 Christstollen..78
 Sweet Shortbread Cookies..80
 Chocolate Muffins...82
 Cinnamon Muffins...83
 Schokocrossies..84
 Butter biscuits...85
 Vanilla crescent cookies..86
 Banana Cinnamon Cookies...87
 Orangentaler..88
 Nut Nougat Cream Cookies..89
 Linz eyes...90
 Marble biscuits...92
 Lemon biscuits..93
 Nougat balls..94
 Oat biscuits...95
 Mini almond corners...96

Cake 98
 Carrot cake...99
 Chocolate cake...100
 Almond cake..102
 Walnut cake...104
 Apple tart...105
 Red wine cake..106
 Bundt cake...108

Desserts 109
 Pear with caramel sauce...110
 Strawberry tiramisu in a glass..111
 Chocolate mousse..112
 Quarkstollen..113

Pana Cotta...............114
Coconut chia pudding...............115
Mulled wine cherry gingerbread mousse...............116
Grilled chocolate banana...............118
Hot Apricots...............119
Grilled banana dessert...............120
Crepes...............121
Strawberry sorbet...............122
Baked banana...............123
Roasted almonds...............124
Coconut milk rice with raspberries...............125
Sweet couscous...............126

Salads...............127
Layered salad...............128
Red Cabbage Salad...............129
White cabbage salad...............130
Egg salad...............131
Bean salad...............132
Beetroot salad...............133
Bulgur salad...............134

Drinks...............135
Jagertee...............136
Delicious orange punch...............137
Appel - Amaretto Punch...............138
Exotic mulled wine...............139
Children's punch...............140
Mulled wine...............141
Spekulatius liqueur...............142
Vanilla Winter Drink...............143
Punch with coffee...............144
White mulled wine...............145
Grog...............146

Baked Apple Punch...147
Eggnog...148
Golden milk...149
Kiwi Banana Smoothie..150

Imprint..151

In advance - information about the recipes

- I have deliberately omitted recipe photos. They would increase the print price of the book enormously and I could not offer this book for this price.
- The baking times given are based on my experience. Please note that deviations may occur more often.
- If you knead the dough with your hands, use cold butter.
- Use room temperature butter with a food processor.
- Instead of butter, vegetable margarine can of course also be used.
- Of course, a fresh spice can also be used instead of powder.

Abbreviations

- FRZ = frozen
- tsp = teaspoon
- tbsp = tablespoon
- ml = millilitre

Soups

RED LENTIL COCONUT SOUP

Ingredients

400 ml coconut milk

700 ml vegetable stock

180 g red lentils, washed and drained

1 onion, diced

1 clove of garlic, pressed

1 carrot, sliced

2 tsp curry powder

2 tablespoons lemon juice

2 pinches pepper

some (rapeseed) oil for frying

Preparation

Heat the oil in a saucepan and sauté the onion, garlic, and curry powder for about 1 minute.
Add the lentils and carrot and steam briefly.
Deglaze with the vegetable stock and add the coconut milk. Then bring to the boil.
Simmer gently for 25 minutes until the lentils break down and the vegetables are soft.
Puree the soup and pass it through a sieve.
Finally, season the soup with lemon juice and pepper.

PUMPKIN SOUP

Ingredients

500 g Hokkaido pumpkin, seeded and diced

700 ml vegetable soup

1 onion, finely chopped

1 clove of garlic, pressed

½ tsp ginger powder

1 pinch nutmeg

2 pinches pepper

1 pinch of salt

3 tbsp (rapeseed) oil

Pumpkin seed oil for drizzling

Preparation

Heat the oil in a saucepan and sauté the onion and garlic.
Add the pumpkin and steam briefly.
Deglaze with the vegetable stock and add the spices.
Bring to the boil and simmer gently for 25 minutes until the pumpkin is soft.
If the pumpkin soup is too thick, add some vegetable stock and bring to the boil again.
Now puree the soup and serve drizzled with pumpkin seed oil.

CHEESE SOUP

Ingredients

100 g grated Gouda

200 g processed cheese

150 g mushrooms, sliced

1 onion, finely chopped

500 ml vegetable stock

500 ml milk

1 tablespoon white wine

2 tbsp flour

2 tbsp oil

2 tablespoons chives

1 tbsp pepper

Preparation

Heat the oil in a saucepan and fry the onion until translucent.

Add the flour and make a classic roux.

Add the vegetable stock and milk and bring to the boil while stirring.

Remove the pan from the heat and stir in the processed cheese.

When the processed cheese has melted, stir in the Gouda.

When the Gouda has melted, bring the soup back to the boil.

Turn off the heat and add the mushrooms, white wine, and pepper.

Leave to infuse for 5 - 10 minutes.

Serve on deep plates and sprinkle with chives.

VEGETABLE CREAM SOUP

Ingredients

5 Potato

400 g vegetables to taste (carrots, kohlrabi, peppers, etc.)

1 onion

1 clove of garlic

700 ml vegetable stock

½ tsp ginger powder

½ tsp pepper

½ tsp salt

2 tbsp (rapeseed) oil

1 tbsp parsley to garnish

Preparation

Cut the vegetables and potatoes into small cubes.

Squeeze the garlic clove and dice the onion.

Heat the oil in a saucepan and sauté the onion and garlic until translucent.

Add the potatoes and vegetables, and fry briefly.

Pour in the vegetable stock, bring to the boil and simmer for 30 minutes.

Puree the soup with a hand blender.

Serve the soup on a plate and garnish with parsley.

TOMATOES - VEGETABLES SOUP

Ingredients

1 can chopped tomatoes

1 can strained tomatoes

3 carrots

1 onion

2 garlic cloves

1 leek

1 spring onion

1 courgette

1 tablespoon sugar

2 tbsp (coconut) oil

Salt to taste

Preparation

Cut the vegetables into small pieces and press the garlic cloves. Heat a pan with oil and fry the onion until translucent.

Add all ingredients except chopped tomatoes and simmer for 5 minutes.

Add the tomatoes to the pot and simmer on low heat for 20 minutes.

Puree the soup and season with salt.

BROCCOLI CREAM SOUP

Ingredients

1 broccoli

4 potatoes

1 onion

1 clove of garlic

800 ml vegetable stock

200 ml coconut milk

2 tbsp (rapeseed) oil

Salt to taste

Preparation

Dice the potatoes, chop the onion and press the garlic clove.
Heat a pot with oil and fry the onion until translucent.

Add the vegetable stock, garlic, and potatoes and cook for 10 minutes in a closed pot.

Meanwhile, cut off the broccoli florets and chop the stems.

Add the broccoli and coconut milk and cook for another 15 minutes.

Season with salt and bring to the boil again briefly.

CAULIFLOWER SOUP

Ingredients

1 cauliflower, in small pieces

1 potato, in small cubes

3 carrots, thinly sliced

2 onions, finely chopped

1 clove of garlic, pressed

700 ml vegetable stock

1 tsp curry powder

½ tsp ginger powder

2 pinches pepper

3 tbsp (rapeseed) oil

1 tbsp parsley to garnish

Preparation

Heat the oil in a saucepan and sauté the onion and garlic until translucent.

Add the cauliflower and carrots and sauté briefly.

Deglaze with the vegetable stock, add the spices and simmer for 20 minutes.

Puree the soup with a hand blender.

If the soup is too thick, add a little water and bring to the boil.

Serve the soup on a plate and garnish with parsley.

BUCKWHEAT - PAPRIKA SOUP

Ingredients

100 g buckwheat

300 g potatoes

1 (red) pepper

1 Carrots

1 onion

1000 ml warm vegetable stock

250 ml cream

2 tbsp (rapeseed) oil

Salt to taste.

Preparation

Peel and wash the potatoes and cut them into small pieces.
Finely chop the onion and cut the pepper and carrot into small pieces.

Heat the oil in a high pan and fry the onion, pepper, and carrot for 3 minutes.

Add the vegetable stock, buckwheat, and potato and simmer for 30 minutes over medium heat.

Add the cream and simmer for another 10 minutes.

Season with salt and serve on deep plates.

BARLEY SOUP

Ingredients

150 g pearl barley (medium)

125 g smoked tofu, diced

5 potatoes, diced

1 small piece of celery, diced

2 carrots

1 onion, finely chopped

½ stick leek, cut into rings

1500 ml vegetable stock

3 tbsp. soy sauce

1 pinch nutmeg

2 pinches pepper

2 tbsp (rapeseed) oil

Parsley to garnish

Preparation

Heat the oil in a saucepan and sauté the onion until translucent.

Add the pearl barley and sauté until translucent.

Add the rest of the vegetables and fry briefly.

Add the vegetable stock, bring to the boil and simmer gently for 30 minutes until the pearl barley is cooked.

Sear the smoked tofu in a frying pan and add to the pot.

Add the spices, bring to the boil and leave to infuse for 5 minutes.

Serve on deep plates sprinkled with parsley.

CHESTNUT CREAM SOUP

Ingredients

400 g chestnuts, coarsely chopped

1000 ml vegetable stock

100 ml white wine

Juice and grated orange

2 onions, diced

1 clove of garlic, pressed

3 tsp fresh thyme

2 tablespoons honey

2 pinches pepper

2 tbsp (rapeseed) oil

Preparation

Heat the oil in a saucepan and fry the onion, garlic, and chestnuts.
Deglaze with honey and white wine and simmer for 5 minutes.
Add the vegetable stock, juice, and zest of the orange and spices.
Simmer gently for 25 minutes until the chestnuts are soft.
Now puree the soup.
Serve on pre-warmed plates.

CELERY - APPLE SOUP

Ingredients

1 small celeriac, finely diced

1 leek, cut into rings

1 onion, diced

1 clove of garlic, pressed

3 apples, variety to taste, peeled, cored, cut into spades.

1000 ml vegetable stock

2 pinches pepper

1 tablespoon lemon juice

100 ml olive oil

Sugar

Cinnamon

some (olive) oil for frying

Preparation

Heat the oil in a saucepan and sauté the onion, garlic, and leek.
Deglaze with the vegetable stock, add lemon juice, 1 tbsp sugar, and pepper and simmer gently for 15 minutes.
Now puree the soup.
While the soup is cooking, glaze the apple slices in olive oil with a little sugar.
Add the apple slices to the soup and serve, dusted with a little cinnamon.

SPICY ORANGE LENTIL SOUP

Ingredients

Juice and grated orange

700 ml vegetable stock

400 ml coconut milk

200 g red lentils, washed and drained

1 onion, diced

1 clove of garlic, pressed

1-2 tsp chilli powder (to taste)

2 tsp curry powder

2 pinches pepper

some (rapeseed) oil for frying

Preparation

Heat the oil in a saucepan and sauté the onion and garlic.
Add the lentils and steam briefly.
Deglaze with the vegetable stock and add the lentils, chilli powder, pepper, curry powder, and coconut milk.
Bring to the boil and simmer gently for 25 minutes until the lentils have broken down.
Add the orange juice and the zest.
Puree the soup and serve on warmed plates.

SWEET POTATO CHICKPEA SOUP

Ingredients

100 g sweet potatoes, diced

240g chickpeas

200 ml cream

1 onion, diced

1 clove of garlic, pressed

400 ml water

1 stock cube

1 tablespoon lemon juice

Pinch of salt

1 tsp pepper

some (rapeseed) oil for sautéing

Preparation

Heat the oil in a saucepan and sauté the onion and garlic clove.

Add the sweet potato and sauté.

Add the stock cubes and deglaze with 400 ml water.

Add the chickpeas and cook the soup for 20 min.

Then add the cream and lemon juice.

Puree the soup well and season with salt and pepper.

CREAM OF MUSHROOM SOUP

Ingredients

100 g mushrooms, sliced

400 ml water

20 ml cream

1 stock cube

1 onion, diced

1 clove of garlic, diced

some (rapeseed) oil for sautéing

3 tbsp flour

½ tsp parsley

1 pinch nutmeg

1 pinch of pepper

some parsley to garnish

Preparation

Heat the oil in a saucepan and sauté the onion and garlic clove.

Add the mushrooms and sauté.

Now sweat the flour in the pot.

Add the stock cube and the water.

Let the soup simmer for 10 minutes, stirring constantly.

Then puree and refine with pepper and nutmeg.

Finally, add the cream and sprinkle with parsley.

POTATO AND LEEK SOUP

Ingredients

700 ml water

1 stock cube

3 potatoes, diced

1 onion, diced

2 leeks, in rings

1 carrot, sliced

50 g ground cashew nuts

3 tablespoons parmesan

2 tsp turmeric

1 pinch nutmeg

1 tsp mustard

some (rapeseed) oil for sautéing

some parsley to garnish

Preparation

Heat the oil in a saucepan and sauté the vegetables.

Add the stock cubes, cashew nuts, Parmesan, and water and simmer for 15 minutes.

Season to taste with the spices and mustard.

Serve the soup garnished with parsley.

Main dishes

PANCAKE

Ingredients (8 pancakes)

200 ml milk

200 g flour

2 eggs

50 g sugar

50 g oil

1 tsp baking powder

1 pinch of salt

some (rapeseed) oil or butter for frying

Preparation

Mix the flour, baking powder, salt, oil, milk, eggs, and sugar in a bowl with a whisk until smooth.

Melt the butter in a pan and stir into the batter.

Heat a teaspoon of oil in a frying pan (not hot!), then pour the batter into the pan with a small ladle.

Fry the pancakes for 2 minutes, turn over and fry again for 1 minute.

Add a little more oil before the next pancake.

Spread or top finished pancakes as desired.

SOUTH TYROLEAN SPINACH DUMPLINGS

Ingredients (6 dumplings)

250 g - 300 g dumpling bread

300 g frozen spinach, drained

2 eggs

250 ml milk

1 onion

1 clove of garlic

1 tbsp flour

1 tsp salt

2 pinches pepper

1 tbsp rapeseed oil

Sauce

200 g butter

2 tablespoons parmesan

Preparation

Put the dumpling bread into a large bowl (cut the bread into small pieces).

Heat the oil in a pan and sauté the onion and garlic.

Add the spinach and bring to the boil.

Add the milk and simmer for 2 minutes over medium heat.

Add the eggs, salt, pepper, and Parmesan and stir well.

Add everything to the dumpling bread in the bowl and leave to cool slightly.

Mix and form dumplings.

Place the dumplings in a pan of lightly simmering salted water for 20 minutes.

Heat the butter slowly in a saucepan.

When the butter is liquid, add the Parmesan.

Put the dumplings on a plate and serve with the sauce poured over them.

SOY SCHNITZEL VIENNESE STYLE

Ingredients

Soy Big Steak(s)

Flour

1 egg

Breadcrumbs

Salt and pepper

1 lemon cut into wedges

(Rapeseed) oil for frying

Preparation

Soy Big Steaks in boiled salted water for 30 minutes.
Then squeeze the water out of the steaks as well as possible!

Prepare three plates: Put some flour in plate 1.

On plate 2, add an egg, season with salt, and pepper, and whisk with a fork.

Put the breadcrumbs in dish 3.

Turn the steaks first in the flour, then in the egg, and finally in the breadcrumbs.

Fry the steaks in a pan heated with sufficient oil until golden brown on both sides.

Finished steaks can be dabbed with some kitchen roll paper.

Serve with lemon wedges and your choice of garnish.

VEGET. MINCED MEAT STEW

Ingredients

150 g soy granules

2 onions, chopped

2 leeks, in rings

1000 ml vegetable stock

250 ml cream

5 tbsp tomato paste

1 tablespoon mustard

1 tsp paprika

1 tsp sugar

1 tsp salt

3 pinches pepper

1 tbsp (rapeseed) oil

Preparation

Prepare the soya granules according to the instructions on the packet. Heat the oil in a pan and fry the onion until translucent.

Add the drained soy granules, leek, tomato paste, vegetable stock, mustard, and spices.

Simmer for 15 minutes, stirring several times.

Stir in the cream, turn off the heat and leave to infuse for another 5 minutes. Bread can be served as a side dish.

TOMATO-LENTIL STEW

Ingredients

2 cans (400g each) peeled tomatoes

200 g onions

400 g aubergines

250 g red lentils

3 garlic cloves

1 tbsp cumin

5 tbsp olive oil

1 tsp cinnamon

1 red chilli pepper

1 tsp sugar

500 ml vegetable stock

2 pinches pepper

3 spring onions

5 stalks parsley

1 tsp lemon juice

possibly a little salt

Preparation

Finely chop the onions and garlic.
Heat two tablespoons of olive oil in a large saucepan.
Sauté the onions and garlic until translucent.

Add the cinnamon, cumin, chilli pepper, and sauté briefly.

Add a teaspoon of sugar and let it caramelise slightly.

Add the vegetable stock and peeled tomatoes, and season with pepper.

Allow the sauce to boil down, uncovered, over medium heat for 20 minutes.

In the meantime, clean the aubergine and cut into 2 cm cubes.

Heat the remaining olive oil in a pan and fry the aubergine on all sides.

Rinse the lentils in a colander and drain.

Add the lentils to the sauce and cook, covered, for 20 minutes.

Add the aubergines 5 minutes before the end of the cooking time.

Clean the spring onions and cut into fine rings.

Pluck off the parsley leaves and chop coarsely.

Season the stew with salt, pepper, sugar, and lemon juice.

Serve with spring onions and parsley.

VEGETABLE - COCONUT STEW

Ingredients

200 ml coconut milk

400 g frozen vegetables to taste (carrots, broccoli, etc.)

100 g frozen leaf spinach

300 ml vegetable stock

1 tbsp (rapeseed) oil

2 pinches nutmeg

Salt and pepper to taste

1 tbsp grated coconut for garnish

Preparation

Bring the vegetable stock to the boil in a large pot and add the frozen vegetables.
Add the oil and nutmeg and simmer for 15 minutes, covered.

Add the coconut milk and bring to the boil briefly.

Season to taste with salt and pepper.

Turn off the heat and let the stew simmer for 5 minutes.

Serve in deep plates garnished with grated coconut.

PASTA PAN WITH MUSHROOMS

Ingredients

250 g durum wheat spaghetti

1 tsp turmeric

1 onion, diced

3 small courgettes, thinly sliced

250 g mushrooms, sliced

1 tsp cumin

1 tbsp curry powder

4 tbsp chives or parsley (fresh or frozen)

2 tbsp soy sauce

(Sesame) oil for frying

Pepper and salt

Preparation

Break (quarter) the spaghetti into four pieces and cook, adding turmeric to the cooking water.
Heat the oil in a saucepan and sauté the onion.
Add the mushrooms and fry for 3 minutes.
Add the courgettes, cumin, curry powder, and fry for 5 minutes.
Add the spaghetti, soy sauce, pepper, chives/parsley, and mix well.

SMOKED TOFU CASSEROLE

Ingredients

200 g smoked tofu

400 tomato pieces (from the can)

50 ml cream

2 onions, diced

3 cloves of garlic, pressed

2 peppers, cut into cubes

1 aubergine, cut into cubes

1 tbsp (rapeseed) oil

1 tsp oregano

Salt and pepper

Preparation

Preheat the oven to 180° C convection oven.
Heat the oil in a pan and sauté the onion and garlic until translucent.

Add the paprika and sauté over a gentle heat for 8 minutes.

Place the warm vegetable mixture together with the tofu and aubergine cubes in a shallow baking dish and mix.

Mix the tomatoes with the cream and season with pepper, salt, and oregano.

Pour over the casserole and leave to simmer in the oven for about 45 minutes.

OVEN VEGETABLES

Ingredients

4 potatoes

1 courgette

2 peppers

2 onions

4 tbsp olive oil

1 - 2 tbsp spices to taste (rosemary, thyme, oregano...)

Salt and pepper to taste

Preparation

Preheat the oven to 180° C convection oven.

Cut the potatoes into wedges. Cut the courgettes into slices. Cut the peppers into strips. Cut onion into rings.

Line a baking tray with baking paper and spread the vegetables evenly on it.

Sprinkle the spices over the vegetables.

Cook in the oven for 30 - 35 minutes.

Allow to cool briefly and serve.

SPINACH - RISOTTO

Ingredients

300 g risotto rice

400 g fresh baby spinach, cut (or frozen spinach, drained)

1 red chilli pepper, deseeded and finely chopped

2 stalks of lemongrass, make a knot from each stalk.

1 onion, chopped

2 cloves of garlic, pressed

1200 ml vegetable stock

300 ml white wine

1 tablespoon lemon juice

some salt and pepper

2 tbsp (olive) oil

Preparation

Heat the oil in a saucepan and sauté the onion, and garlic.
Add the rice and stir well.

After 1 minute, add the white wine, and simmer.

Add the lemongrass knots, then gradually add the vegetable stock and cook the risotto for 15 minutes, stirring constantly.

Remove the lemongrass and add the spinach leaves.

Simmer for a further 5 minutes, stirring constantly. (Until the spinach has collapsed).

Season with lemon juice, salt, and pepper.

PUMPKIN RAGOUT

Ingredients

½ Hokkaido pumpkin

250 ml milk

2 tbsp flour

1 tbsp parmesan

1 pinch nutmeg

2 tbsp (rapeseed) oil

Salt

Preparation

Cut the washed and seeded pumpkin into pieces of about 2 x 2 cm. Heat the oil in a saucepan and sauté the pumpkin.

Stir in the flour until it has combined with the oil.

Slowly add the milk. Stir diligently to prevent lumps from forming.

Add the Parmesan and season with salt and nutmeg.

Simmer on low for 15 minutes, stirring occasionally, until the pumpkin cubes are soft.

BAKED APPLE STRUDEL WITH VANILLA SAUCE

Ingredients

For the dough

250 g flour

100 ml lukewarm water

1 Egg

1 pinch of salt

For the filling

1200 g apples, peeled and cored

50 g marzipan paste

5 tbsp lemon juice

3 tbsp almond slivers

1 tsp cinnamon

2 tablespoons orange juice

Vanilla sauce

600 ml vanilla flavoured milk

3 tbsp cornflour

Preparation

Knead all the ingredients for the dough, adding the water slowly to make a firm, elastic dough.

Wrap in cling film and leave to rest for an hour.

Preheat the oven to 180°C.

Cut 400 g of apple into quarters and place on a baking tray lined with baking paper. And brush with a little lemon juice, sprinkle with almonds and marzipan.

Bake in the oven for 12 minutes.

Cut the remaining apples into thin slices, mix with the remaining lemon juice and cinnamon and leave to infuse.

Roll out the dough into a rectangle, spread it out on a large kitchen towel, and dust well with flour.

Roll out the dough so thinly that the pattern of the cloth shows through.

Lightly mash the baked apples together with the marzipan and almonds with a fork and mix with the marinated apples.

Spread the apple mixture evenly over the pastry, leaving a 3 cm border.

Fold in the "short" sides of the pastry rectangle up to the filling.

Roll up from the long side with the help of the kitchen towel.

Now place the strudel on the tray with the help of the kitchen towel so that the seam is at the bottom.

Bake in the oven for 45 minutes.

For the custard, take a few spoonfuls of the milk and mix with the cornflour.

Bring the remaining milk to the boil, stir in the mixed powder and bring to the boil again briefly.

LENTIL-PARANUT ROAST

Ingredients

250 g red lentils

300 g Brazil nuts

400 ml water

1 onion

120 g breadcrumbs

2 garlic cloves

1 carrot

1 bay leaf

1 tbsp. soy sauce

1 tablespoon tomato paste

1 tablespoon oregano

2 tbsp (rapeseed) oil for frying

some butter for greasing

Side dish: Rice

Preparation

Preheat the oven to 180 °C.
Bring the lentils and bay leaf to the boil in a pan with 400 ml water.

Cook for 25 minutes.

Remove the bay leaf and set the lentils aside.

Heat the oil in a frying pan.

Sauté the chopped onion, crushed garlic cloves, and chopped carrot for 3 minutes.

Coarsely chop one-third of the Brazil nuts. Finely grind the remaining Brazil nuts.

Put the sautéed onion mixture in a bowl with the ground and chopped Brazil nuts.

Add the lentils, breadcrumbs, tomato paste, soy sauce, and oregano, and mix well.

Place in a baking dish greased with butter.

Bake in the oven for 25 minutes.

Leave to cool slightly.

Remove carefully and serve with rice.

COCONUT SPAGHETTI

Ingredients

500 g spaghetti

600 ml coconut milk

700 ml vegetable stock

4 peppers

4 carrots

2 onions

2 tbsp curry

Pepper and salt to taste

Preparation

Cut the peppers and carrots into small cubes.

Put all the ingredients, except the spaghetti, in a pan and bring to the boil.

Simmer on a medium heat for 5 minutes.

Add the spaghetti and cook according to the instructions on the packet until al dente.

Season to taste with salt and pepper.

BAKED BEANS

Ingredients

2 cans white beans

400 g strained tomatoes

3 tbsp tomato paste

1 onion

1 clove of garlic

3 tablespoons sugar

1 tbsp (rapeseed) oil

Salt

Pepper

Chilli powder

Preparation

Preheat the oven to 180° C.

Squeeze the garlic clove and chop the onion.

Heat the oil in a pan and fry the onion and garlic until translucent.

Place the beans with the strained tomatoes in a casserole dish.

Add the sautéed onion with the garlic and the rest of the ingredients to the casserole dish and mix well.

Bake in the oven for 30 minutes.

POTATO GRATIN

Ingredients (2 servings)

500 g potatoes

125 g cream

80 ml milk

150 g grated cheese

A little margarine to grease the casserole dish

Salt

Pepper

Nutmeg

Preparation

Preheat the oven to 180° C convection oven.
Grease the casserole dish with a little butter.

Peel and wash the potatoes and cut into thin slices.

Layer the potato slices in the prepared dish, seasoning each layer with salt, pepper, and nutmeg.

Mix the cream with the milk and add.

Spread the grated cheese over the gratin.

Bake in the oven for approx. 45 minutes until the potatoes are soft and the liquid is absorbed.

PICHELSTEINER

Ingredients

40 g soy cubes (dry product)

400 g potato, sliced

200 g kohlrabi, sliced

200 g carrots, sliced

200 g celery, sliced or diced

1 leek, in rings

1 onion, chopped

3 tbsp (rapeseed) oil

1000 ml vegetable stock

Salt, pepper and nutmeg

4 tbsp parsley to garnish

Preparation

Bring the soy cubes to the boil in the vegetable stock and leave to infuse for 10 minutes. Remove the soy cubes from the vegetable broth with a sieve.

Set aside the vegetable stock.

Heat the oil in a pot and add the onion, leek, potato, kohlrabi, celery, carrots, and soy cubes in layers.

Season each layer lightly with salt, pepper, and nutmeg.

Pour over the vegetable stock until the vegetables are ¾ covered.

Cover and simmer for 30 minutes over medium heat. Do not stir! When the potatoes are firm to the bite, stir, and serve garnished with parsley.

GRILLED CORN ON THE COB

Ingredients

4 corn on the cob
50 g butter
1 tbsp herb mixture to taste
Some (rapeseed) oil

Preparation

Pre-cook the corn on the cob for about 15 minutes and leave to cool slightly.

Preheat the grill and brush the grate with oil.

Pierce the corn on the cob lengthwise with a skewer and brush with a little butter and season with the herb mixture.

Place the corn on the cob on the grill and grill evenly for about 10 minutes.

RICE - MEATBALLS

Ingredients

150 g rice

2 eggs

150 g Emmental, grated

2 onions, finely chopped

2 carrots, grated

1000 ml vegetable stock

3 tbsp. herbs (to taste)

Breadcrumbs

(Rapeseed) oil or clarified butter for frying

Salt and pepper to taste

Preparation

Bring the vegetable stock to the boil, add the rice and simmer for 15 minutes. Drain the rice and leave to cool.

In a bowl, mix together the rice, cheese, carrots, eggs, and onions.

Stir in pepper, salt, herbs, and breadcrumbs until the meatball dough has a good consistency.

Leave the dough to swell for 15 minutes.

Form the meatballs and roll again in breadcrumbs.

Heat the oil in a frying pan and fry the meatballs over medium heat until golden brown on both sides.

Serve with the desired side dish. Also delicious as a burger in a bun.

WINTER RATATOUILLE

Ingredients

1 can (400 g each) peeled tomatoes

4 carrots

100 ml water

150 g aubergine

100 g couscous

1 clove of garlic

2 tbsp (rapeseed) oil

1 tsp curry powder

1 pinch of sugar

Some salt

Preparation

Clean the aubergine and cut into 1.5 cm cubes.

Heat one teaspoon of oil in a large non-stick frying pan.

Fry the aubergine until light brown and season with salt.

In the meantime, peel and slice 4 carrots.

Place the aubergine on a plate.

Sauté the carrots in the pan with 1 tsp oil.

Finely chop the garlic clove, add with the curry powder and steam briefly.

Add the tomatoes and 100 ml water, bring to the boil, season with salt and 1 pinch of sugar.

Cook over a gentle heat for 10 minutes.

Pour 150 ml of boiling water over the couscous with a little salt in a bowl.

Cover and leave to soak for at least 5 minutes.

Mix the aubergines into the sauce.

Heat briefly and serve with couscous.

CHICKPEA CURRY

Ingredients

1 tin chickpeas (400 g)

1 can coconut milk (400 ml)

100 ml white wine

1 onion, finely chopped

2 cloves of garlic, pressed

2 tablespoons parmesan

2 tbsp curry

1 tbsp. soy sauce

1 tsp sugar

3 tbsp (rapeseed) oil

Side dish: Rice

Preparation

Heat the oil in a saucepan and sauté the onion and garlic until translucent.

Deglaze with white wine and simmer a little.

Slowly stir in the coconut milk.

Add the curry, parmesan, soy sauce, sugar, and chickpeas.

Simmer on medium heat for 10 minutes.

Serve the chickpea curry with rice.

POTATO GOULASH

Ingredients

250 g mushrooms, in pieces

2 potatoes, diced

1 onion, finely chopped

2 cloves of garlic, pressed

2 red peppers, diced

2 tsp tomato paste

1 tsp caraway

1 tsp marjoram

1 tsp salt and 1 tsp pepper

2 tsp paprika

3 pinches chilli powder

4 tbsp (rapeseed) oil for frying

Water to cover the potatoes

Preparation

Heat 2 tbsp oil in a large saucepan and fry the onion until translucent.

Add the tomato purée, potato, paprika, and garlic.

After 3 minutes, add water so that the potatoes are covered.

Add the remaining ingredients and simmer for 10 minutes until soft.

Heat the remaining oil in a pan and fry the mushrooms until golden brown.

Stir in the mushrooms and serve in warmed plates.

POTATO - CARROT RÖSTI

Ingredients (8 Rösti)

200 g potatoes

200 g carrots

2 tablespoons milk

1 tablespoon cornflour

½ tsp lemon juice

Pinch of nutmeg

3 tbsp (rapeseed) oil

Salt

Preparation

Peel the potatoes and carrots and grate them coarsely with a kitchen grater.

Mix with milk, cornflour, lemon juice, salt, and nutmeg.

Heat the oil in a frying pan.

Use round cutters to form 8 equally sized hash browns in the pan.

Remove the cutters and fry the rösti on both sides until golden brown.

KOHLRABI POTATO VEGETABLES

Ingredients

1 kg kohlrabi

2 carrots

2 potatoes

100 ml cream

1 tsp salt

3 pinches pepper

3 pinches nutmeg

1 tsp vegetable stock

3 tablespoons butter

Boiling water

Preparation

Cut the kohlrabi, potatoes and carrots into cubes.

Cook the vegetables with the salt in a pot of water until soft.

Pour off the water.

Mix with the rest of the ingredients and puree.

GRILLED PEPPER SKEWERS

Ingredients

1 each of red, yellow, orange and green peppers.
10 rosemary sprigs
1 tbsp garlic powder
2 tablespoons honey
250 ml olive oil
Salt and pepper

Preparation

Cut the peppers into bite-sized pieces and stick them on the rosemary sprigs.

Mix the olive oil, honey, salt, pepper, and garlic powder, and marinate the pepper skewers for 30 minutes.

Preheat the grill and brush the grate with oil.

Grill the pepper skewers for approx. 12 minutes, turning regularly.

SPAGHETTI WITH PEANUT SAUCE

Ingredients

300 g spaghetti

800 ml vegetable stock

120 g roasted peanuts

1 pepper, finely diced

1 carrot, finely diced

3 onions, finely chopped

3 cloves of garlic, pressed

1 piece ginger

1 tablespoon sugar

2 tablespoons lemon juice

2 tbsp peanut butter

1 tsp coriander

1 tbsp soy sauce

2 tbsp (olive) oil for frying

Preparation

Heat the oil in a saucepan and fry the onion and garlic until translucent.

Add all ingredients except lemon juice and coriander and simmer until the spaghetti is al dente.

Add the coriander and lemon juice.

Mix well again and serve.

GRILLED MUSHROOM SKEWERS

Ingredients

500 g cleaned mushrooms
4 cloves of pressed garlic
4 tbsp soy sauce
2 tablespoons honey
1 tsp oregano
1 tsp thyme
2 tbsp olive oil
½ tsp pepper

Preparation

Preheat the grill and coat the grid with oil.

Mix garlic with oil, soy sauce, pepper, honey, oregano, and thyme to make a marinade add mushrooms to marinade

Divide the mushrooms on skewers and place on the grill.

Grill until done, turning regularly.

PAPRIKA - COUSCOUS

Ingredients

300 ml vegetable stock

200g couscous

2 peppers

1 tablespoon tomato paste

2 tbsp soy sauce

2 tbsp curry paste (red or yellow)

2 tbsp white wine vinegar

2 tbsp (olive) oil

Salt, pepper, chilli

Preparation

Heat the curry paste with the vegetable stock in a saucepan and bring to the boil.

Add the couscous and remove the pan from the heat.

Allow the couscous to swell.

Wash, seed and dice the peppers and add to the couscous later.

Stir together the tomato paste, soy sauce, and vinegar, and add to the couscous and pepper mixture.

Add salt, pepper and chilli and season to taste.

STUFFED MUSHROOMS

Ingredients (4 servings)

250 g mushrooms

80 g grated cheese

150 g cream cheese

1 onion, finely diced

1 pepper, finely diced

2 tbsp (olive) oil

Paprika powder

Pinch of pepper

½ tsp salt

Preparation

Preheat the oven to 180° C convection oven.
Line a baking tray with baking paper.

Clean the mushrooms and cut out the insides.

Heat the oil in a pan and sauté the inside of the mushrooms.

Add the cream cheese, paprika, onion, and spices.

Fill this mixture into the mushrooms and cover with the grated cheese.

Place the mushrooms on a baking tray lined with baking paper.

Bake in the oven for 15 - 20 minutes.

FRIED TOFU

Ingredients

400 g tofu

400 ml coconut milk

60 g ginger

2 garlic

1 lime

2 tsp sugar

2 tsp paprika

½ tsp salt

3 tbsp (rapeseed) oil

Preparation

Cut the tofu into pieces about 1 cm wide and 4 cm long.

Chop the ginger and garlic cloves.

Mix with coconut milk, juice of 1 lime, sugar, paprika, and salt.

Place the tofu in the marinade and leave to marinate for at least 2 hours.

Remove the tofu from the marinade and pat dry.

Heat the oil in a pan and fry the tofu for 5 minutes.

Sweets - Cookies

WAFFLES

Ingredients

250 g flour

200 ml milk

120 g butter

70 g sugar

3 eggs

2 tsp baking powder

1 sachet vanilla sugar

Oil to grease the waffle iron

1 pinch of salt

Preparation

Mix the butter and sugar until creamy.

Stir in the eggs one by one.

Mix the flour with the vanilla sugar, salt and baking powder and stir in alternately with the milk.

Grease the waffle iron with oil.

For one waffle, place 2-3 tbsp of waffle batter in the centre of the waffle iron.

Bake the batter in the waffle iron until golden brown.

Leave the finished waffles to cool on a cooling rack.

Top the finished waffles as desired.

MARZIPAN POTATOES

Ingredients (50 potatoes)

For the dough

200 g marzipan paste

200 g icing sugar

1 tsp water

1 pinch of salt

For decorating

2 tbsp cocoa powder

1 pinch cinnamon

Preparation

Warm the marzipan slightly.

Knead with the icing sugar, salt, and water.

Form the marzipan into balls the size of cherries.

Sieve the cocoa with the cinnamon onto a plate and roll the marzipan balls in it.

Put the balls into a fine sieve and shake briefly to shake off excess cocoa powder.

MOCHA COOKIES

Ingredients (15 pieces)

130 g sugar

130 g butter

130 g flour

½ tsp baking powder

1 tablespoon instant espresso powder

50 g fine oat flakes

1 pinch of salt

Preparation

Preheat oven to 180°C.

Mix the flour, sugar, baking powder, and cocoa.

Dissolve the espresso powder in 1 tbsp boiling water and stir in.

Add the butter and oat flakes and work into a soft dough.

Form 15 balls and flatten a little on a baking tray lined with baking paper. Make sure there is a little space between them.

Bake in the oven for 15 minutes.

CINNAMON STARS

Ingredients (about 50 stars)

For the biscuit dough

200 g icing sugar

2 tablespoons cinnamon

8 tbsp. water

1 tablespoon lemon juice

200 g ground hazelnuts

200 g ground almonds

1 tbsp grated orange zest

1 pinch of salt

Flour for the work surface

For the cast

150 g icing sugar

Some water

1 tsp cinnamon

Preparation

Preheat oven to 180°C.

Mix all the ingredients together except the flour.

Dust the work surface with flour. If the dough is too sticky, simply add some more flour.

Roll out the dough to about 1 cm thick.

Cut out stars with the biscuit cutter and place on a baking tray lined with baking paper.

Bake the cinnamon stars in the preheated oven for about 7 minutes.

While the cinnamon stars are still soft, place them on a wire rack to cool.

For the icing, simply mix all the ingredients together and brush the stars with it.

NUT BISCUITS

Ingredients (about 40 biscuits)

For the dough

300 g flour

2 sachets custard powder

100 g tender oat flakes

150 g ground hazelnuts

120 g sugar

½ packet baking powder

200 g butter

½ tsp cinnamon

6 tbsp. water

some icing sugar for decorating

To coat

100 g sour cherry jam

Preparation

For the dough, first mix all the dry ingredients in a bowl. Knead with butter and water to form a shortcrust pastry.

If necessary, add a little water or flour until the dough is no longer sticky but can be kneaded well.

Place the dough in the fridge for 30 minutes.

Preheat the oven to 180°C.

Roll out the dough in portions on the floured work surface to a thickness of 5 mm and cut out using cookie cutters.

Bake in the oven for 15 minutes.

Leave the biscuits to cool.

In the meantime, heat the sour cherry jam and pass through a sieve.

Spread half of the biscuits with the jam and place a dry biscuit on top.

Dust with icing sugar to finish.

MARZIPAN NOUGAT PRALINES

Ingredients

For the dough

200 g marzipan paste

150 g icing sugar

175 g nougat

1 pinch of salt

For decorating

50 g coarsely chopped pistachio kernels

200 g dark chocolate

Preparation

Warm the marzipan slightly.
Knead with icing sugar.

Roll out the marzipan between two layers of baking paper to a rectangle 5mm thick.

Heat the nougat over a bain-marie until it is spreadable.

Spread evenly over the marzipan.

Roll up the marzipan sheet from the long side into a roll.

Place in cling film in the fridge for 2 hours.

Melt the dark chocolate.

In the meantime, cut bite-sized pieces from the marzipan roll and shape into a chocolate ball.

Dip this marzipan nougat praline into the chocolate.

Sprinkle the top with pistachios and leave to cool.

SHORTBREAD BISCUITS

Ingredients

500 g flour

250 g sugar

250 g butter

1 Egg

1 egg yolk

½ packet baking powder

2 packets vanilla sugar

1 pinch of salt

Preparation

Put all the ingredients in a bowl and knead into a dough.

Leave to rest in the fridge for one hour.

Preheat the oven to 180°C.

Make any desired biscuits with piping bag.

Place the biscuits on a baking tray lined with baking parchment.

Bake for about 15 minutes.

COCONUT MACAROONS

Ingredients (40 pieces)

250 g grated coconut

220 g sugar

4 egg white

1 pinch of salt

(Optional baking wafers)

Preparation

P preheat oven to 180°C.

Line two baking trays with baking paper.

Beat the egg whites until stiff.

Mix the grated coconut, sugar, lemon juice, and salt, and carefully fold into the beaten egg white.

Take small portions with a teaspoon and place on the baking paper.

(Optionally place on round baking wafers)

Bake the coconut macaroons in the preheated oven for about 18 minutes until they turn light golden brown.

Leave to cool on a cooling rack.

CHOCOLATE PRALINES

Ingredients (50 chocolates)

For the dough

200 g dark chocolate

60 g ground almonds

80 g cream

4 tbsp orange juice

1 tsp grated orange zest

1 pinch of salt

For decorating

300 g dark chocolate

Preparation

Heat the cream and dissolve 200 g of chocolate in it.

Stir in the orange juice, grated orange zest, and almonds.

Leave to cool in the fridge for 5 hours.

Grate 100g of chocolate.

Melt 200g of chocolate.

Cover the balls with the liquid chocolate.

Put the grated chocolate in a small bowl and roll the balls in it.

SPECULOOS

Ingredients (10 speculoos)

200 g flour

100 g butter

80 g sugar

1 pinch of salt

1 tablespoon milk

2 tbsp gingerbread spice

Preparation

Mix together the flour, sugar, salt, and gingerbread spice.

Add the butter and milk and knead into a dough.

Leave the dough to rest in the fridge for 30 minutes, wrapped in cling film.

On a floured work surface, roll out the dough to about 5 mm thick.

Preheat the oven to 180°C.

Using a pizza cutter and a ruler, cut the dough into even rectangles.

Decorate rectangles with patterns as desired.

Carefully lift the speculoos and place them on a baking tray lined with baking paper.

Bake in the oven for 8 minutes.

SIMPLE GINGERBREAD

Ingredients

300 g flour

180 g icing sugar

100 g honey

2 eggs

½ tbsp baking cocoa

1 tsp bicarbonate of soda

3 tsp gingerbread spice

2 pinches of cinnamon

Preparation

Preheat the oven to 180° C.

Mix all the dry ingredients in a bowl.

Add the honey and eggs, and knead into a dough.

Then roll out the dough, cut out the gingerbread, brush with egg white, and decorate with sprinkles as desired.

Bake the gingerbread for about 8-10 minutes.

Allow to cool and serve.

CHOCOLATE GINGERBREAD

Ingredients

300 ground hazelnuts

3 eggs

80 g soft butter

100 g sugar

100 g chocolate shavings

4 drops bitter almond flavouring

1 cl rum

2 tbsp flour

1 tsp baking powder

1 tbsp gingerbread spice

Wafers, dark chocolate coating, and sugar sprinkles

Preparation

Preheat the oven to 180° C.

Cream together the butter, sugar, and eggs.

Add the eggnog and rum, add the remaining ingredients gradually, and mix well.

If the dough sticks too much, add 1 tablespoon more flour.

With a spoon, prick the gingerbread out of the dough and place on a baking tray lined with baking paper.

Bake the gingerbread for approx. 20 minutes. Leave to cool and decorate with melted chocolate coating and coloured sprinkles.

PEPPERNUTS

Ingredients

250 g flour

175 g butter

150 g sugar

1 tsp cocoa powder

1 packet vanilla sugar

1 tsp cinnamon powder

½ tsp pepper

2 pinches nutmeg

1 pinch of salt

Preparation

Put all the ingredients in a bowl and knead into a dough.

Leave to rest in the fridge for one hour.

Preheat the oven to 180°C.

Form the dough into rolls and cut 1 cm thick slices.

Place on a baking tray lined with baking paper.

Bake for approx. 10 minutes.

After cooling, you can coat the peppernuts with chocolate or sugar icing.

CHRISTSTOLLEN

Ingredients

500 g flour

1 sachet dry yeast

130 g sugar

1 pinch of salt

1 tablespoon lemon zest

200 g butter

250 ml milk

150 g sultanas

100 g ground almonds

100 g marzipan

some icing sugar

2 tablespoons butter

Preparation

Mix all the ingredients (except the sultanas and marzipan) together and knead into a dough.

Leave the dough to rise in a warm place for 2 hours.

Preheat the oven to 180°C.

Pull the dough apart a little, sprinkle the sultanas on top and knead the dough into a ball again.

Then roll out the dough into a rectangle (approx. 30 x 25 cm) and roll up from the longer side.

Shape the marzipan into a sausage shape, approximately the length of the pastry.

Bake the stollen for 15 minutes.

Reduce the temperature to 160°C and bake for a further 45 minutes.

After cooling, brush the Christmas stollen with 2 tbsp melted margarine.

Sprinkle with plenty of icing sugar and serve.

SWEET SHORTBREAD COOKIES

Ingredients

For the dough

300 g flour

100 g sugar

200 g cold butter

1 egg

1 packet vanilla sugar

1 pinch of salt

some flour for the work surface

For decorating

150 g icing sugar

Some water

Sugar/chocolate sprinkles

Preparation

Put all the ingredients in a bowl and knead together.

Wrap the dough in cling film and leave to rest in the fridge for an hour.

Preheat the oven to 180°C.

Roll out the dough with a rolling pin on a floured work surface to a thickness of 5 mm.

Cut out the biscuits with biscuit cutters and place on a baking tray lined with baking paper.

Bake the biscuits in the preheated oven for about 10 minutes until golden.

Leave to cool on a cooling rack.

For the icing, simply mix icing sugar with a little water.

Spread the icing on the biscuits and decorate with sprinkles.

To store, it is best to put them in a biscuit tin.

CHOCOLATE MUFFINS

Ingredients

300 g flour

250 g sugar

50 g cocoa powder

1 package baking powder

7 tbsp rapeseed oil

350 ml water

1 pinch of salt

Muffin - paper cups

Preparation

Preheat the oven to 180° C convection oven.

Mix the flour with the cocoa powder, baking powder, sugar, salt, oil, and water.

Pour the batter into small muffin paper cups and bake for approx. 30 minutes.

CINNAMON MUFFINS

Ingredients (12 muffins)

For the dough

100 g tender oat flakes

250 ml milk

80 g butter

400 g flour

1 sachet vanilla sugar

40 g yeast (1 packet dry yeast)

For the filling

50 g butter

4 tablespoons honey

1 tablespoon cinnamon

Preparation

Mix all the ingredients together and knead into a dough.

Leave to rise in a warm place for one hour.

Roll out the dough into a rectangle on the floured work surface.

For the filling, melt the butter with honey.

Coat the pastry with the mixture and dust with cinnamon.

Roll up the rectangle and cut 2cm thick slices.

Place each one in a muffin tin and leave to rise for another 20 minutes.

Preheat the oven to 180°C. Bake in the oven for 12 minutes.

SCHOKOCROSSIES

Ingredients

100 g cornflakes

200 g dark chocolate

Preparation

Melt the chocolate in a bain-marie.

When the chocolate has melted completely, stir in the cornflakes.

Line a baking tray with baking parchment.

Using a teaspoon, place small portions on the baking tray and refrigerate until the chocolate crispies are firm.

BUTTER BISCUITS

Ingredients (30 pieces)

300 g flour

150 g butter

150 g icing sugar

1 egg

1 packet vanilla sugar

1 tsp baking powder

1 tsp lemon juice

1 pinch of salt

some sugar for decoration

Preparation

Preheat oven to 180°C.

Knead all the ingredients into a dough.

Put some sugar on a plate.

Shape a tablespoon of dough into a ball and press one side into the sugar.

Place the balls, sugared side up, on a baking tray lined with baking paper.

Bake the biscuits in the preheated oven for about 20 minutes until golden.

Leave to cool on a cooling rack.

VANILLA CRESCENT COOKIES

Ingredients

For the dough

275 g flour

200 g butter

100 g ground almonds

75 g sugar

50 g icing sugar

2 egg yolk

2 packets vanilla sugar

1 pinch of salt

Preparation

Put the flour, almonds, sugar, butter, egg yolks, vanilla sugar, and salt in a bowl and knead into a dough.

Wrap the dough in cling film and place in the fridge for an hour.

Preheat the oven to 180° C convection oven.

Flour the work surface and shape the dough into rolls approx. 1.5 cm thick.

Cut the rolls into 4 cm long pieces and shape into croissants.

Place the croissants on a baking tray lined with baking parchment.

Put the croissants in the oven for about 10 minutes.

Sift icing sugar over the still warm crescents.

Leave to cool and store in a sealable container.

BANANA CINNAMON COOKIES

Ingredients (40 pieces)

300 g flour

50 g ground almonds

100 g butter

100 g sugar

1 banana

2 tablespoons cinnamon

1 tsp baking powder

2 tablespoons milk

Preparation

Mash the banana and knead into a dough with all the ingredients.

Leave the dough to rise for 10 minutes.

Preheat the oven to 180°C.

Roll out the dough and cut out biscuits with biscuit cutters.

Place the biscuits on a baking tray lined with baking paper.

Bake in the oven for 15 minutes.

ORANGENTALER

Ingredients (40 pieces)

For the dough

200 g flour

100 g ground almonds

200 g butter

150 g sugar

1 sachet custard powder

½ grated orange zest

75 g chopped dark chocolate

1 tsp baking powder

2 tablespoons orange juice

For garnishing

75 g sugar

Preparation

Mix all the dry ingredients in a bowl.

Knead the butter and orange juice into a smooth dough.

Put the dough in the fridge for 30 minutes.

Preheat the oven to 180°C.

Form the dough in portions into a 4 cm thick roll.

Roll the rolls in sugar and cut into 5 mm thick slices.

Bend the pieces into croissants and place them on a baking tray lined with baking paper. Bake in the oven for 10 minutes.

NUT NOUGAT CREAM COOKIES

Ingredients

200 g nut nougat cream

150 g flour

1 egg

1 tsp baking powder

Icing sugar for sprinkling

Preparation

Preheat the oven to 180°C.

Knead all the ingredients into a dough.

Form small biscuits or balls from the dough and place on a baking tray lined with baking paper.

Bake for about 12 minutes and leave to cool.

Sprinkle with icing sugar.

LINZ EYES

Ingredients (80 pieces)

300 g flour

200 g butter

110 g icing sugar

80 g ground almonds

5 tbsp milk

1 tsp vanilla sugar

grated zest of half a lemon

1 pinch cinnamon

150 g jam for filling

Preparation

Mix all the dry ingredients in a bowl.

Add the milk and margarine to the flour mixture in batches.

Mix all the ingredients well and knead into a dough.

Cover the dough airtight and let it rest in the fridge for an hour.

Pre-heat the oven to 180 °C.

Then knead the dough once more.

Roll out the dough to a thickness of four millimetres on a floured work surface.

Cut out biscuits with biscuit cutters (it is important that the biscuit cutters are large enough so that you can still poke one or two holes in the biscuit).

Cut out small holes in half of the vegan biscuits - the jam will show through here later.

Place the biscuits on a baking tray lined with baking paper and bake in the preheated oven for 8 minutes until golden brown.

Leave the biscuits to cool.

Stir the jam until smooth and spread it on the biscuit halves without the hole.

Put the linzer eyes together.

MARBLE BISCUITS

Ingredients (50 pieces)

300 g flour

200 g butter

130 g sugar

1 tbsp. vanilla custard powder

1 tsp baking powder

2 tbsp cocoa powder

2 tablespoons water

Preparation

Knead all the ingredients, except the cocoa powder, into a shortcrust pastry.

Divide the dough in half and knead one half with cocoa powder.

If the dough is dry, add a little more water.

Roughly knead both halves of the dough together to create a nice grain.

Wrap the dough in cling film and refrigerate for one hour.

Preheat the oven to 180°C.

Form the dough in portions into rolls of approx. 4 cm diameter.

Cut slices approx. 1 cm thick with a sharp knife.

Place the slices on a baking tray lined with baking paper.

Bake in the oven for 12 minutes.

LEMON BISCUITS

Ingredients (50 pieces)

250 g flour

120 g cold butter

130 g sugar

3 eggs

1 packet vanilla sugar

1 tsp baking powder

Grated lemon and juice of one lemon

1 pinch of salt

Preparation

Knead all the ingredients into a dough.

Form the dough into a ball and place in the fridge for at least one hour.

Preheat the oven to 180°C.

Roll out the dough to a thickness of 1 cm on a floured work surface and cut out the biscuits with biscuit cutters.

Place the biscuits on a baking tray lined with baking parchment.

Bake in the oven for about 12 minutes.

NOUGAT BALLS

Ingredients

200 g flour

100 g cold butter

80 g sugar

100 g hazelnut brittle

70 g nut nougat, in small cubes

1 egg

½ tsp salt

Preparation

Preheat oven to 180°C.

Knead the flour, sugar, salt, butter, and egg into a dough.

Form small balls from the dough and place a nougat cube in the middle. Enclose the nougat cube with the dough.

Roll the small balls in the brittle and place on a baking tray lined with baking paper.

Bake for about 15 minutes and then leave to cool.

OAT BISCUITS

Ingredients (30 pieces)

100 g butter

120 g seeded oat flakes

100 g flour

120 g sugar

1 sachet vanilla sugar

½ teaspoon baking powder

50 g chopped almonds

Preparation

Preheat oven to 180°C.

Melt the butter for the dough.

Stir in the oat flakes and leave to cool slightly.

Add the remaining ingredients and knead into a soft dough.

Using two teaspoons, place small portions on a baking tray lined with baking paper and flatten them slightly.

Bake in the oven for 15 minutes.

MINI ALMOND CORNERS

Ingredients (70 pieces)

For the dough

200 g butter

400 g flour

100 g sugar

2 tablespoons milk

half a bottle of almond flavouring

For the topping

50 g candied orange peel

200 g chopped almonds

50 g sliced almonds

100 g ground almonds

80 g sugar

100 g butter

200 ml milk

Additionally

80 g apricot jam

150 g dark chocolate

Preparation

Preheat the oven to 180°C.

Mix all the ingredients for the dough.

Wrap the dough in cling film and leave to rest in the fridge for 30 minutes.

Roll out the dough thinly on a baking tray lined with baking paper.

Spread the apricot jam evenly on top.

Chop the candied orange peel.

Toast the candied orange peel, the chopped and the sliced almonds in a well heated pan until golden brown, stirring frequently.

Add the ground almonds, sugar and butter. Stir and turn off the cooker.

Stir in the milk.

Pour this nut mixture onto the prepared pastry and spread evenly.

Bake in the oven for 25 minutes.

Leave to cool and cut into even squares.

Then, using a sharp knife, divide the squares crosswise to create almond corners.

Coat the corners of the almond wedges with melted dark chocolate and allow the chocolate to harden.

Cake

CARROT CAKE

Ingredients

250 g carrots

200 g ground nuts (to taste)

1 apple

130 g flour

100 g sugar

1 package baking powder

1 tsp cinnamon

½ tsp cardamom

130 ml milk

100 ml (rapeseed) oil

For the glaze:

Mix 100 g icing sugar with 2 tbsp lemon juice

Preparation

Preheat the oven to 180°C.

Mix all the dry ingredients, including the spices.

Add the milk and oil and mix quickly with the dry ingredients.

Finely grate the carrots and apple and fold in.

Pour the batter into a greased springform pan lined with baking paper and bake in the oven for approx. 45 minutes.

After cooling, coat with the icing sugar glaze.

CHOCOLATE CAKE

Ingredients

For the dough

250 g flour

250 g sugar

130 ml oil

180 ml milk

3 eggs

3 tbsp cocoa powder

1 sachet baking powder

1 packet vanilla sugar

For the decoration

150 g dark chocolate

2 tbsp icing sugar

Preparation

Preheat oven to 180°C.

Beat the eggs, sugar, oil and vanilla sugar until frothy.

Mix the flour, cocoa powder, baking powder, and milk, and add.

Preferably with a hand mixer, work into a smooth batter.

Pour the batter into a springform pan lined with baking paper.

Bake in the oven for 45 minutes.

Allow the cake to cool slightly in the tin, then cool on a cooling rack and spread with chocolate icing.

ALMOND CAKE

Ingredients

For the dough

100 g sugar

200 g butter

300 g flour

1 tbsp. vanilla custard powder

1 sachet vanilla sugar

6 tbsp honey

2 tablespoons water

For the filling

200 g almonds

120 g icing sugar

1 sachet vanilla sugar

2 tablespoons water

1 tablespoon honey

Preparation

For the dough, first mix all the dry ingredients in a bowl.

Knead with butter, honey and water to form a shortcrust pastry.

If necessary, add a little water or flour until the dough is no longer sticky but can be kneaded well.

Place the dough in the fridge for one hour.

Preheat the oven to 180°C

For the filling, heat all the ingredients in a saucepan, but do not boil.

Allow to cool.

Line the base of a springform pan lined with baking paper with half of the dough and draw a rim about 1.5 cm high.

Spread the almond mixture over the pastry base.

Roll out the rest of the dough and place it as a lid over the filling.

Prick several times with a fork.

Bake in the oven for 35 minutes.

WALNUT CAKE

Ingredients

200 g soft butter

180 g sugar

4 eggs

150 g flour

150 g finely chopped walnuts

1 tsp baking powder

40 ml milk

Couverture

chopped walnuts

Preparation

Preheat oven to 180°C.

Beat the butter and sugar until fluffy and slowly add the eggs.

Mix the flour, finely chopped walnuts and baking powder and stir in alternately with the milk.

Pour the dough into a greased springform pan and bake for approx. 40 minutes. Leave the cake to cool.

Melt the chocolate coating and cover the cake with it.

Decorate with a few walnuts.

APPLE TART

Ingredients

For the dough

80 g butter, a little more for greasing

250 g sugar

150 g flour, a little more for flouring

50 ml water

1 tsp vanilla sugar

For the topping

1 kg apples

40 g sugar

10 g butter

Preparation

Preheat oven to 180°C.

Grease and flour the tart tin (Ø 26cm).

Mix all the dough ingredients in a bowl and knead into a dough.

Roll out the dough on a lightly floured work surface and line the tart tin with it.

Peel and core the apples, cut into thin slices, and spread over the pastry in a fan shape.

Sprinkle with sugar and spread the butter on top.

Bake in the oven for 35 minutes.

RED WINE CAKE

Ingredients

For the dough

200 g margarine

250 g flour

150 g chocolate flakes

125 ml red wine

50 g chopped hazelnuts

4 eggs

200 g sugar

1 sachet vanilla sugar

1 sachet baking powder

2 tsp cocoa powder

1 tsp cinnamon

1 tsp rum

For decorating

Icing sugar for dusting

Preparation

Preheat oven to 180°C.

Beat the eggs until frothy.

Add the sugar and vanilla sugar and continue to beat until fluffy.

Add the margarine while stirring.

Add the remaining ingredients one by one and mix.

Pour the dough into a well-greased loaf tin.

Bake in the oven for approx. 40 minutes.

Test the cake with a chopstick to make sure it is cooked through.

Transfer the cake to a cooling rack and leave to cool.

Sprinkle with icing sugar.

You can also prepare the cake in muffin tins as party snacks.

BUNDT CAKE

Ingredients

For the dough

400 g sugar

some butter for greasing

350 g flour and a little more to flour a springform pan

2 tsp baking powder

1 tsp bicarbonate of soda

1 sachet vanilla sugar

60 g grated coconut

500 ml milk

250 g berries of your choice with 1 tsp salt

For decorating

Icing sugar for dusting

Preparation

Preheat oven to 180°C.

Grease and flour a 24 cm cupcake tin with butter.

Mix the baking powder, baking soda, flour, vanilla sugar, sugar, and coconut flakes.

Add the milk and oil and mix until smooth. Fold in the salt and berries.

Pour the batter into the springform pan and bake in the oven for 60 minutes.

Leave to cool slightly and turn out onto a cooling rack.

Dust the cooled cupcake with icing sugar.

Desserts

PEAR WITH CARAMEL SAUCE

Ingredients (4 servings)

For the pears

4 pears

100 ml white port wine

400 ml white wine

50 g sugar

1 tablespoon cinnamon

1 sachet vanilla sugar

For the caramel sauce

100 ml boiling water

60 g sugar

Preparation

Peel the pears and carefully cut out the core.

Bring all the ingredients to the boil in the saucepan.

Put in the pears and simmer for 4 minutes.

Cover the pot and leave to cool.

For the caramel sauce, caramelise the sugar in a saucepan and deglaze with 100 ml boiling water.

Remove the pears from the wine broth and place on a plate.

Pour the caramel sauce over the top and serve.

Strain the wine broth. Can be used as a drink with this.

STRAWBERRY TIRAMISU IN A GLASS

Ingredients

700 g strawberries

150 g biscuits (Amarettini - or chopped lady fingers)

150 g cream

350 g curd

70 g sugar

some amaretto

Preparation

Chop strawberries into small pieces.

Pour a little amaretto over the biscuits.

Whip the cream and stir in the quark with the sugar.

Place a few biscuits in the glass, then spread a layer of cream on top.

Spread the strawberries over the cream.

Pour some cream over the strawberries and decorate with 1-2 biscuits.

Leave to infuse in the fridge for 2 hours.

Also very tasty with raspberries!

CHOCOLATE MOUSSE

Ingredients (4 servings)

200 g dark chocolate

1 egg

1 egg yolk

1 tsp brandy

400 g cream

Fruits to garnish

Preparation

Melt chocolate in a water bath.

Beat the egg with the egg yolk in a bowl in a hot water bath until foamy.

Fold in the chocolate and brandy with a whisk.

Whip the cream until stiff and fold into the lukewarm mousse.

Divide the mousse between bowls and place in the fridge for an hour.

Serve garnished with fresh fruit.

QUARKSTOLLEN

Ingredients (4 servings)

500 g flour

250 g curd

250 g sultanas

170 g sugar

130 g ground almonds

170 g butter

3 eggs

1 package baking powder

1 bottle rum flavouring

Grated lemon

4 drops bitter almond flavouring

1 pinch nutmeg

1 packet vanilla sugar

1 pinch of salt

Preparation

Knead all the ingredients together into a dough and place in a stollen tin.

Bake the stollen at 180°C, in a preheated oven at 18°C for about 60 minutes.

Then brush with a little (rapeseed) oil and dust thickly with icing sugar.

PANA COTTA

Ingredients (4 servings)

500 ml cream

50 g honey

5 sheets gelatine

1 sachet vanilla sugar

200 g raspberries (frozen or fresh)

Preparation

Soak the gelatine in cold water.

Combine the remaining ingredients, except the raspberries, and place in the saucepan. Bring slowly to the boil and simmer for 5 minutes.

Remove the pot from the cooker.

Remove the gelatine from the water, squeeze out well, and add to the pot.

Now stir until the gelatine has completely dissolved.

Pour the pana cotta into small jars and place in the fridge for at least 3 hours.

Puree the raspberries, add a little sugar if desired, and pour over the firm pana cotta.

Of course, strawberries can also be used.

COCONUT CHIA PUDDING

Ingredients (2 servings)

200 ml coconut drink

8 tbsp chia seeds

½ tsp vanilla sugar

2 tablespoons sugar

2 tbsp chopped dark chocolate

Preparation

Mix the coconut drink with the vanilla sugar.

Stir in the chia seeds

Add all the remaining ingredients, mix well and chill.

Leave to soak for 40 minutes. Stir occasionally.

Serve well chilled.

MULLED WINE CHERRY GINGERBREAD MOUSSE

Ingredients (4 servings)

For the mousse

400 g silken tofu

200 g dark chocolate

3 packets vanilla sugar

1 tbsp gingerbread spice

5 tbsp milk

3 tbsp boiled espresso

For the mulled wine cherries

200 g morello cherries

200 ml mulled wine

1 tsp cinnamon

3 tablespoons honey

1 tablespoon cornflour

Preparation

Melt the chocolate with the espresso over a water bath.

Puree the silken tofu with the milk, gingerbread spice, and vanilla sugar.

Mix everything together and place in the fridge.

Drain the morello cherries and collect the juice.

Heat the mulled wine in a saucepan.

Add the honey and cinnamon, and simmer for 5 minutes.

Mix cornflour in 4 tbsp juice and add to the simmering mulled wine.

Add the morello cherries.

Layer the gingerbread mousse with the mulled wine cherries in glasses.

GRILLED CHOCOLATE BANANA

Ingredients

4 bananas

100 g chocolate

2 tablespoons lemon juice

Some (rapeseed) oil

Preparation

Preheat the grill and coat the grid with oil.

Cut the skin of the bananas and the flesh lengthwise on the upper side.

Squeeze the lemon juice over the pulp.

Break the chocolate and fill it into the bananas.

Place the bananas with the skin side on the grill and grill until the chocolate melts.

HOT APRICOTS

Ingredients

3 large apricots, halved and pitted

A little grated nutmeg

2 tablespoons honey

Preparation

Preheat the oven to 200°C convection oven.

Place the apricot halves with the cut sides in a baking dish.

Pour honey and nutmeg over the apricots and bake in the oven for about 15 minutes.

GRILLED BANANA DESSERT

Ingredients for 2 desserts

2 bananas

2 scoops vanilla ice cream

Chopped peanuts in caramel

Preparation

Preheat the grill.

Grill the bananas, in their skins, over a medium heat for about 10 minutes, turning frequently.

Cut the bananas lengthwise on a plate and flatten with a fork.

Add the vanilla ice cream and serve garnished with the chopped peanuts in caramel.

CREPES

Ingredients for 6 crepes

100 g flour
200 ml milk
1 shot sparkling mineral water
Nutmeg
1 pinch of salt
(Rapeseed) oil for frying

Preparation

Mix all the ingredients, except the oil, into a smooth batter, and leave to soak for 10 minutes.

Brush a pan with oil and heat.

Pour a portion of the batter into the pan and spread it around the pan.

Fry the pastry on both sides until light brown.

STRAWBERRY SORBET

Ingredients (4 servings)

600 g strawberries, frozen

70 g sugar

300 ml water

2 lemons

Preparation

Squeeze the lemons into a bowl.

Bring the water, sugar and 6 tbsp lemon juice to the boil in a saucepan.

Stir until the sugar has dissolved.

Leave the lemon syrup to cool.

Finely purée the strawberries with the syrup.

Season to taste with the remaining lemon juice.

Place in the freezer for 15 minutes.

Shape the strawberry sorbet with an ice cream scoop and serve.

BAKED BANANA

Ingredients (2 servings)

2 bananas

2 tbsp chia seeds

1 tablespoon honey

1 tbsp breadcrumbs

1 pinch cinnamon

1 pinch vanilla sugar

(Coconut) oil for frying

Preparation

Cut the peeled bananas in half lengthwise.

Coat the bananas with honey.

Mix the remaining ingredients together, except for the oil.

Roll the bananas in the mixture.

Heat the oil in a frying pan and fry the bananas in it.

Serve the baked bananas garnished with chia seeds.

ROASTED ALMONDS

Ingredients

200 g almonds

50 ml water

50 g sugar

1 packet vanilla sugar

1/2 tsp cinnamon

1 pinch of salt

Preparation

In a heated pan, bring the water, sugar, vanilla sugar, and cinnamon to the boil.

Add the almonds and stir frequently. When the sugar starts to become crumbly, continue stirring. The sugar must melt and draw threads.

Place the almonds on a baking tray lined with baking paper and leave to cool. The almonds must lie separately, otherwise they will stick together.

COCONUT MILK RICE WITH RASPBERRIES

Ingredients (4 servings)

For the rice pudding

100 g rice

1 tsp grated lemon zest

2 tablespoons sugar

500 ml low-fat coconut milk

1 tsp cinnamon

1 sachet vanilla sugar

For garnishing

150 g raspberries

Preparation

Bring all the rice pudding ingredients except the rice to the boil in the saucepan.

Add the rice and cook over a low heat, stirring occasionally.

Leave to soak for 40 minutes.

Puree the raspberries and pass through a kitchen sieve.

Fill the coconut milk rice into glasses and garnish with the raspberry puree.

SWEET COUSCOUS

Ingredients (4 servings)

400 g couscous, prepared according to the package instructions

8 dates (pitted)

1 pomegranate

5 tbsp sultanas

Hot water for swelling the sultanas

4 tbsp flaked almonds

3 tablespoons butter

3 tbsp orange juice

4 tsp cinnamon

2 tablespoons honey

1 pinch of salt

4 tbsp icing sugar for garnish

Preparation

Put the sultanas in a bowl and pour hot water over them and leave to soak.

Remove the red fruit seeds from the pomegranate and cut the dates into eighths.

Toast the flaked almonds in a pan without fat until light brown.

Stir the butter into the finished couscous.

Drain the sultanas and leave to drain.

Mix all the ingredients, except the icing sugar, with the couscous.

Portion into small, warmed bowls and serve dusted with icing sugar.

Salads

LAYERED SALAD

Ingredients (4 servings)

2 lettuce hearts

2 peppers

200 g defrosted frozen peas

2 onions

1 jar of celery cutlets

3 eggs

1 jar mayonnaise

2 tablespoons sugar

150 g grated cheese

Preparation

Cut lettuce hearts into strips, chop peppers, finely dice onions, dice eggs.

Put all the ingredients in a bowl in the order given in the list of ingredients.

Leave to infuse in the fridge for at least 12 hours, preferably overnight.

RED CABBAGE SALAD

Ingredients (4 servings)

½ head red cabbage

300 g carrots

1 apple

4 tbsp lime juice

6 tbsp orange juice

4 tbsp (rapeseed) oil

1 tsp salt

½ teaspoon curry powder

Preparation

Clean the carrots and apples, core the apples.

Clean the red cabbage and cut it into large pieces.

Put all the ingredients in the blender.

Chop coarsely for 4 seconds on low and push down with a spoon.

Chop again for 4 seconds on medium speed.

WHITE CABBAGE SALAD

Ingredients (4 servings)

½ white cabbage

3 carrots

1 tbsp white wine vinegar

1 tbsp (rapeseed) oil

½ tsp salt

½ tsp pepper

Chives to garnish

Preparation

Cut the white cabbage into fine strips and finely grate the carrots.

Mix all the ingredients together.

Garnish with chives and leave in the fridge for 2 hours.

EGG SALAD

Ingredients (4 servings)

9 eggs

200 g mayonnaise

Salt and pepper

Chives to garnish

Preparation

Hard boil the eggs in boiling water for 10 minutes.

Then rinse the eggs in cold water, peel, and shell them.

Mix the mayonnaise, lemon juice, and eggs.

Season to taste with salt and pepper.

Garnish with chives and leave in the fridge for 2 hours.

BEAN SALAD

Ingredients (4 servings)

1 can white beans

1 apple

1 orange

1 onion

2 tsp mustard

1 tsp thyme

1- 2 tbsp white wine vinegar

4 tbsp (rapeseed) oil

½ tsp pepper

½ tsp salt

Preparation

Pour the beans into a sieve, rinse well and drain.

Put the beans in a salad bowl.

Cut the orange and apple into small pieces, finely dice the onion.

Mix the orange, apple, onion, and thyme with the beans.

In a separate bowl, mix the oil, vinegar, mustard, salt, and pepper, and pour over the salad.

Leave the salad to stand in the fridge for one hour.

BEETROOT SALAD

Ingredients (4 servings)

1 package beetroot, cooked and peeled

1 handful walnuts

1 handful dried plums

1 clove of garlic

1 tsp salt

1 tsp sugar

Preparation

Press the garlic clove and grate the beetroot.

Mix all the ingredients together.

Leave to infuse in the fridge for at least 2 hours.

BULGUR SALAD

Ingredients (4 servings)

1 bunch spring onions

300 g bulgur

300 ml tomato juice

300 ml water

3 tablespoons parsley

4 tbsp peanuts

1 pinch cinnamon

1 pinch of pepper

1 pinch of salt

7 tbsp (rapeseed) oil

Preparation

Cut the spring onion into fine rings.

Heat the oil in a frying pan and sauté the spring onion.

Add the bulgur and fry for 2 minutes over a medium heat.

Add the water, tomato juice, salt, and pepper.

Simmer the bulgur for 10 minutes, covered, over a low heat.

Toast the peanuts in a frying pan.

Sprinkle with cinnamon and fry.

Mix the parsley and peanuts into the bulgur, and serve hot.

Drinks

JAGERTEE

Ingredients for 1,5 l

500 ml black tea, prepared according to package instructions
500 ml red wine
150 ml brown rum
250 ml orange juice
Juice of one lemon
1 orange, sliced
6 cloves
1 cinnamon stick

Preparation

Pour black tea, red wine, orange juice, cinnamon, and cloves into a saucepan and heat, but do not boil!

When the mixture is hot, add the rum, lemon juice, and orange slices.

Heat again until just before boiling. Turn off the heat and leave the Jagertee to infuse for a few hours.

Heat again before serving.

DELICIOUS ORANGE PUNCH

Ingredients for 1 l punch

1000 ml orange juice
2 cinnamon sticks
1 clove
1 star anise
200 ml cream
1 sachet vanilla sugar
1 sachet cream stiffener
1 untreated orange

Preparation

First put the orange juice in a saucepan. Season the orange juice with cinnamon, cloves, and star anise. Heat the whole thing gently.

In the meantime, prepare the cream. Whip the cream with the vanilla sugar, the cream stiffener, and the orange zest until stiff.

Then fill the punch into glasses and cover with the creamy whipped cream. The punch is best served nice and warm.

APPEL - AMARETTO PUNCH

Ingredients

1000 ml apple juice
1 apple, cored and cut into small cubes
Peel of an orange
1 cinnamon stick
8 tbsp amaretto

Preparation

Warm all the ingredients, except the amaretto, gently in a saucepan for 15 minutes.

Pour into cups and add one to two tablespoons of amaretto to taste.

EXOTIC MULLED WINE

Ingredients for 6 cups

1 litre red wine

2 sticks cinnamon

3 cloves

1 orange, sliced

Juice of one lemon

3 tablespoons honey

1 tablespoon sugar

Some fresh ginger

A dash of white rum

Preparation

Heat all the ingredients in the pot, but do not let them boil.

Mulled wine is best served nice and warm.

CHILDREN'S PUNCH

Ingredients for 6 punch glasses

500 ml water
500 ml apple juice
1 litre elderberry juice
4 oranges, sliced
Grated lemon zest of one lemon
1 cinnamon stick
4 cloves

Preparation

Bring water to the boil in the saucepan.

Add the lemon zest, cinnamon, and cloves and turn off the heat.

In the second saucepan, slowly heat the apple and elderberry juices. The juices must not boil! Add the orange slices and turn off the heat.

After about 10 minutes, carefully pour the pots together and leave to infuse for a few hours.

Reheat before serving.

MULLED WINE

Ingredients for 6 cups

1000 ml red wine
1 orange, sliced
2 sticks cinnamon
3 cloves
Sugar to taste

Preparation

Heat all the ingredients in the pot, but do not let them boil.

Mulled wine is best served nice and warm.

SPEKULATIUS LIQUEUR

Ingredients

150 ml grain
250 ml whipped cream
50 g icing sugar
3 tbsp. nut nougat cream
2 tsp Spekulatius spice mix

Preparation

Grain, nut nougat cream, spice mixture, and icing sugar, mix well together.

Whip the cream until creamy and stir in.

Store the speculoos liqueur in the fridge and use within 2 months.

VANILLA WINTER DRINK

Ingredients for 2 cups

100 g cashew nuts (soaked overnight)
350 ml almond drink
4 tablespoons honey
1 tsp cinnamon
1/2 tsp nutmeg
1 tsp vanilla sugar

Preparation

Blend all the ingredients together and bring to the boil in a saucepan.

Stir occasionally and simmer gently for a few minutes.

Pour into cups while still warm and enjoy.

PUNCH WITH COFFEE

Ingredients for 4 cups

800 ml hot coffee

2 teaspoons grated orange zest

2 pinch cinnamon

2 pinch clove powder

2 pack vanilla sugar

12 cl liqueur (to taste)

4 orange slice for garnish

Preparation

Mix all the ingredients together, except the liqueur, and leave to infuse briefly.

Pour the punch into cups and add the liqueur (to taste).

Garnish the punch with orange slices and serve immediately.

WHITE MULLED WINE

Ingredients for 6 cups

1.5 litre white wine
1 orange
150 ml orange juice
80 ml rum
4 cloves
4 tablespoons sugar

Preparation

Heat all the ingredients slowly in the pot, but do not let them boil.

Remove the cloves before serving.

Serve the white mulled wine nice and warm.

GROG

Ingredients for 1 jar

150 ml water
5 cl rum
2 tsp honey
1 squeeze lemon juice

Preparation

Pour boiling water into a cup.

Add rum, honey, and lemon juice

Serve the grog nice and warm.

BAKED APPLE PUNCH

Ingredients

700 ml apple juice (clear)

800 ml white wine

2 apples, halved and cored

3 cloves

2 cinnamon sticks

Peel grated from one lemon

2 tbsp sugar

50 ml amaretto

1 packet vanilla sugar

Preparation

Preheat the oven to 180° C.
Put the apple juice, wine, lemon zest, vanilla sugar, and spices in a saucepan, and bring to the boil.
Simmer gently for 35 minutes.
Remove the cinnamon sticks and cloves.
While the apples are cooking, sprinkle the cut surfaces of the apples with sugar and place in a buttered baking dish and bake for about 30 minutes.
Add the amaretto to the punch and bring to the boil again.
Put the apples in a punch glass, pour the punch over them and serve.

EGGNOG

Ingredients

1 bottle of egg liqueur (750 ml)

500 ml white wine

500 ml orange juice

1 packet vanilla sugar

Preparation

Put all the ingredients in a saucepan and heat, but do not boil.

GOLDEN MILK

Ingredients for 2 glasses

250 ml milk

1 tbsp turmeric

1 tsp coconut oil

2 pinches ginger

½ tsp cinnamon

1 pinch nutmeg

1 pinch of pepper

Possibly honey (sweeten to your own taste)

Preparation

Mix all the ingredients together.

Heat together in a saucepan, but do not boil.

KIWI BANANA SMOOTHIE

Ingredients for 2 glasses

1 ripe banana

2 ripe kiwis

250 ml coconut drink

1 tbsp lemon juice (preferably freshly squeezed)

Preparation

Mix all ingredients together for about one minute.

Imprint

© Nadia Uzhakhova

2022

ISBN: 9798355887780

1st edition

Contact: Markus Mägerle/ Am Kreisgraben 17/ 93104 Riekofen/ Germany

Printed in Great Britain
by Amazon